History and activities of
Ancient China

Jameson Anderson

www.heinemann.co.uk/library
Visit our website to find out more information about Heinemann Library books.

To order:
☎ Phone 44 (0) 1865 888066
  Send a fax to 44 (0) 1865 314091
📄 Visit the Heinemann Bookshop at www.heinemann.co.uk/library to browse our
💻 catalogue and order online.

First published in Great Britain by Heinemann Library, Halley Court, Jordan Hill, Oxford OX2 8EJ, part of Harcourt Education. Heinemann is a registered trademark of Harcourt Education Ltd.

Editorial: Audrey Stokes
Design: Kimberly R. Miracle in collaboration with Cavedweller Studio
Picture research: Mica Brancic
Production: Vicki Fitzgerald

Origination: Chroma Graphics
Printed and bound in China by WKT Company Limited

13-digit ISBN 978 0431080864 (hardback)
11 10 09 08 07
10 9 8 7 6 5 4 3 2 1

13-digit ISBN 978 0431080949 (paperback)
12 11 10 09 08
10 9 8 7 6 5 4 3 2 1

British Library Cataloguing in Publication Data
Anderson, Jameson
Ancient China. – (Hands on ancient history)
1. China – Civilization – To 221 B.C. – Juvenile literature
2. China – History – To 221 B.C. – Juvenile literature
I. Title
931
A full catalogue record for this book is available from the British Library.

Acknowledgements
The author and publishers are grateful to the following for permission to reproduce photographs: AKG Photos, p. **10** (Erich Lessing); Alamy Images pp. **6** (Panorama Stock Photos Co Ltd), **18** (Eddie Gerald); Ancient Art and Architecture Collection, pp. **9** (R. Sheridan), **12** (Danita Delimont), **15**, **20** (R. Sheridan), **24**; Art Archive, p. **13** (Topkapi Museum Istanbul/ Dagli Orti); Art Directors and Trip, p. **17** (Tibor Bognar); Art Resource, NY, p. **11** (Werner Forman); Bridgeman Art Library, pp. **11**, **16**, **28**; Corbis, pp. **7** (Lowell Georgia), **8** (Jose Fuste Raga), **14** (Asian Art and Archaeology Inc.); Harcourt, pp. **19** (David Rigg), **27** (David Rigg)

Cover photographs of Lao Tse astride a bull (foreground) reproduced with permission of Art Resource, NY/ Snark and the Great Wall of China (background) reproduced with permission of Corbis.

The publishers would like to thank May-lee Chai, Eric Utech and Kathy Peltan for their assistance in the preparation of this book.

Every effort has been made to contact copyright holders of any material reproduced in this book. Any omissions will be rectified in subsequent printings if notice is given to the publishers.

Table of Contents

Some words are shown in bold, **like this**. You can find out what they mean by looking in the glossary.

Chapter 1: Nomads, farmers, and inventors

The Chinese **civilization** began more than 5,000 years ago. It is older than any other civilization. The ancient Chinese made many advances in science, arts, and learning. They invented things such as paper, maths, and fireworks. Many of their inventions are still used today.

Dynasties

At first, the people of ancient China were **nomads**. They moved around a lot. They hunted animals and gathered berries. Later, people settled on farms. Kings and emperors ruled ancient China. They were organized into **dynasties**. Most dynasties were made up of powerful families. These families joined together with other families in the area. They agreed to help protect each other against enemies.

In 221 BCE a man named Qin Shi Haungdi became the first emperor of China. His dynasty lasted until 207 BCE. The Han dynasty took over in 206 BCE and lasted until AD 220. Other dynasties continued to rule China until 1912. China's civilization lasted for thousands of years. This makes it hard to decide where ancient China ends and modern China begins. This book covers the period from the Xia Dynasty until about 100 BCE.

Timeline

1700–1500 BCE Xia Dynasty	**1500–1122 BCE** Shang Dynasty	**1040–221 BCE** Zhou Dynasty

551 BCE Confucius is born

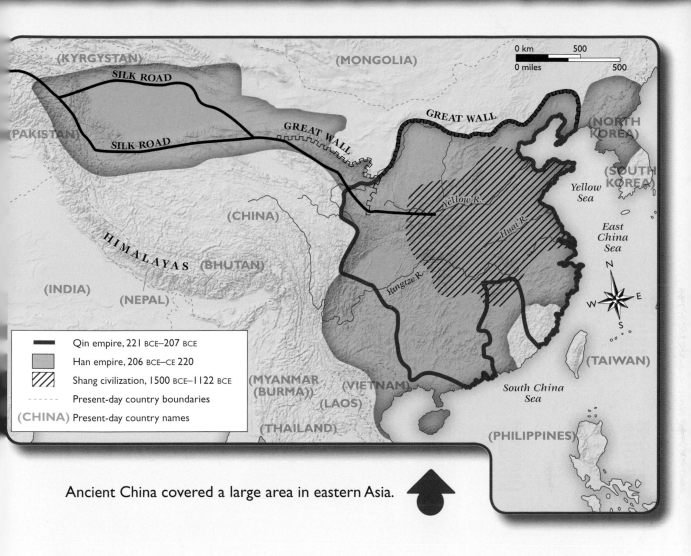

Ancient China covered a large area in eastern Asia.

Map legend:
- Qin empire, 221 BCE–207 BCE
- Han empire, 206 BCE–CE 220
- Shang civilization, 1500 BCE–1122 BCE
- Present-day country boundaries
- (CHINA) Present-day country names

221 BCE–207 BCE

Qin Dynasty

105 BCE

The Chinese invent silk

100 BCE

The Chinese invent paper

BCE means "Before the Common Era", a time before Christianity was a widespread religion. The term "BC" is also used for this time period.

Xia dynasty

For years, no one was certain that the Xia **dynasty** existed. There were Chinese myths and stories about the Xia, but no physical evidence. Then, in 1959, **archaeologists** found objects from the Xia dynasty.

Historians now believe the Xia dynasty ruled China from 1700 to 1500 BCE. The Xia were farmers who used bronze weapons. They also made pottery. Xia rulers often guided people's religious beliefs, as well as ruled. They regularly prayed to spirits for guidance.

Objects found in 1959 led to the discovery of the Xia dynasty.

The Shang and Zhou dynasties

Like the Xia, the Shang dynasty was once believed to be a myth. The Shang came into power in 1500 BCE. They are credited by some with inventing writing. Symbols that stood for words were carved into bones and shared between people of the dynasty. The Shang also carved symbols into turtle shells. Most of the writing was based on the group's beliefs.

Shang dynasty rulers were also religious leaders. The Shang people believed that their kings could talk to the gods. They worshipped the Shang Di, a god who they believed controlled other gods, such as the gods of the sun, moon, wind, and rain.

About 30 kings ruled throughout the Shang dynasty. When kings were buried, hundreds of their soldiers were killed and placed in burial tombs with them. The last king, Di Xin, did not take care of his people well. He took money from them and left them to fend for themselves.

A new dynasty began to emerge from across the western borders of the Shang dynasty. The Zhou dynasty was formed from **nomads** who were friendly to other people. As people of the Shang dynasty became angry with their leader Di Xin, the Zhou dynasty grew.

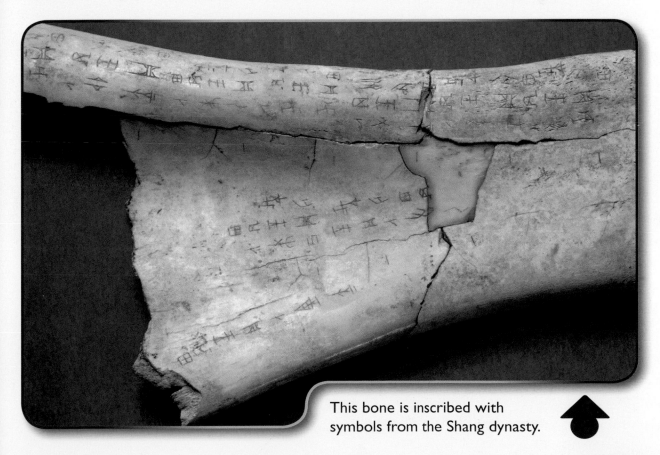

This bone is inscribed with symbols from the Shang dynasty.

The Zhou dynasty lasted from 1040–221 BCE. The last part of the Zhou dynasty (445–221 BCE) is known as the "warring period" because of a series of wars between different Chinese states. Despite the wars, this was a great time for philosophers. Schools of thought such as Confucianism, Taoism, and Legalism emerged from this time. Some of the most memorable Chinese poetry was also written at this time.

In 221 BCE, the Qin, a dynasty located in the western part of China, became dominant. The Qin united the other states. For the first time, China became a unified empire.

Great Wall of China

The Great Wall of China was originally built in small sections by groups of farmers who wanted to keep land to themselves. Early sections of the wall were made of stone.

As farmers expanded their land, and new emperors came into rule, the walls were rebuilt and extended. The Qin emperor ordered that the walls be connected to form one great wall that curves 6,700 kilometres (4,161 miles) from east to west across northern China. Along the wall are watchtowers where the emperor's men watched for enemies.

Today, visitors from around the world come to see the Great Wall of China.

Philosophy

Philosophers told people what the world means and how people should react to the world. Confucianism, Taoism and Legalism were the three main schools of **philosophy** to emerge from the Zhou dynasty.

Confucianism:
Confucius was born in 551 BCE. He believed that everyone should be happy with where they are in life. Confucius said that everyone is born good and has a duty to take care of each other.

Taoism:
Tao means, "the way". Taoists believe that everything in nature works together. That is "the way". They believe that anyone who follows "the way" will live a balanced life.

Legalism:
Legalists believed that the government should establish harsh rules and a stronger moral code as an example for all people to follow.

In this art from ancient China, philosophers share lessons with young people.

Chapter 2: Life in ancient China

Farm life

Many ancient Chinese were **nomads**. They moved from place to place to find animals to hunt and berries to pick. When animals moved or wild berries ran out, families had to move to where there was more food.

Later, the Chinese began setting up farms. They changed from a nomadic to a more settled lifestyle. Most farms were run by extended families. Everyone in the family worked together. They grew wheat, rice, or millet. Most farming was done with hand tools. Some wealthy farmers could afford to use oxen ploughs.

Most families could live off their crops. However, emperors charged **taxes** to the farmers. A family who could not afford to pay their taxes could be forced to work on another farm.

Farming was a way of life in ancient China. Most families supported themselves by raising crops.

Village markets

Some adults made crafts to sell at markets. Each village had a market where craft makers sold their products.

Silk was an important product. Silk makers sold and traded their product with other Chinese and with visitors from other lands. Silk was used to make clothes for nobles and wealthy people.

 People who lived in ancient Chinese cities often worked and traded in the markets.

 Women in ancient China made silk from the cocoons of silk worms.

How silk was made

Silk is made from moth larvae called silk worms. In ancient China, women kept silk worms to use their cocoons to form thread. Silk thread appears when a silkworm's cocoon is boiled. The women wove this thread into cloth. A legend says that silk was discovered by accident when a cocoon fell into an emperor's wife's tea. When she pulled the cocoon from the hot water, silk thread was exposed.

11

Paper

Around 100 BCE the Chinese invented paper. The first paper was very expensive. It was made of silk fibres squeezed together.

Soon paper could be made by mashing plants and rags with water and pressing them together. This made paper cheaper.

Paper was first used by nobles in the government. They already understood the written language. The nobles wrote messages from the emperor on paper and took them to villages. This meant that information could be read to peasants. The nobles who could read had more power than the peasants.

Homes

Housing in China changed a lot during ancient times. Early **nomads** lived in straw huts on the ground in the middle of the countryside.

Later, the ancient Chinese built homes on farms and villages. Homes in villages were made of

Those in ancient China who understood the written language had the most power.

wood and bamboo. Fire could spread quickly from house to house. In cities, several families lived together in one large house. People slept on mats on the floor in southern China. In northern China they slept on platforms. Warm coals were put under the platforms to keep the sleeper warm in the winter.

Families built several buildings on farms. These buildings were used to store crops and hold animals.

Clothing

The people of ancient China wore mostly long, plain clothes known as tunics. The tunics were often made of fibres found in plants such as hemp. Men and women both wore trousers under their tunics.

Nobles in ancient China wore more luxurious clothes. They wore long silk robes. The robes were decorated with inks and dyes made from plants. Sometimes patterns were painted on to the robes, while at other times they were sewn into the fabric.

Nobles in ancient China wore brightly coloured clothing.

Dancing

Street performers entertained the crowds in villages in ancient China. Musicians, dancers, and acrobats entertained people in the cities. They also performed for the emperors and nobility.

Dancing was very popular. Young girls danced on top of round balls. They wore brightly coloured costumes. They often twirled ribbons while they danced. The ancient Chinese played bells and chimes. These made music for the girls to dance to.

Dancing occurred during festivals. Dancing was also used to celebrate the New Year or the emperor's birthday. Many religious ceremonies involved dancing. Groups of dancers toured from village to village to perform.

This sculpture shows the importance of dancing in ancient China.

Music in ancient China was considered spiritual.

Music

There was always music with the dancing. Music was taken more seriously than dancing in ancient China. The ancient Chinese believed that music had special powers. Some people thought that music could affect a person's behaviour. Some music could make people do good things. Other music could make people do bad things.

The most common musical instruments in ancient China were bronze bells. Other instruments included drums, chimes, and flutes.

Sports

Children and adults both played sports. The ancient Chinese often played a game similar to football. Noble men and women also played a version of polo. Like modern-day polo, the game was played on horseback. Players decorated their horses' tails with ornaments. Leaders used the game to get to know each other. The Chinese versions of football and polo were both used as training exercises for the Chinese military.

The most common sport was hunting. It was a very exciting sport. It was also a useful way of catching food. The ancient Chinese used birds that were trained to hunt. Nobility and peasants both hunted for rabbits and pheasants.

 Horses such as the one shown in this sculpture were used to play a form of polo.

The ancient Chinese enjoyed playing board games.

Games

The ancient Chinese played board games and card games. Some games were very similar to ones that are played today. Games were played on holidays, such as the New Year or the emperor's birthday.

Many games and sports in ancient China started during other activities. Hunters practised throwing spears and knives. This practice sometimes turned into a competition.

Other sports grew out of army training. Emperors always wanted their armies to be stronger. They ordered warriors to fight against each other. Crowds gathered when the warriors fought. The wrestling between warriors became a form of entertainment.

Warriors also competed in horse races and stone-throwing contests.

Chapter 4: Hands-on ancient history

By doing the hands-on activities and crafts in this chapter, you will get a feel for what life was like for people who lived and worked in ancient China.

Recipe: Moon cakes

The ancient Chinese celebrated the changing of the seasons. Harvest moon, or mid-autumn festivals have been celebrated in ancient China since the Tang dynasty. The festival celebrates the brightest moon of the year. Today, Chinese families still prepare foods such as moon cakes to celebrate the new moon.

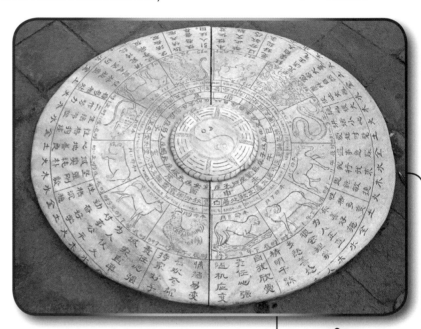

Ancient Chinese stones like this one show calendar markings.

Ingredients and supplies
- home-made dough or tube of ready-made dough
- rolling pin
- one small jar of jam, or other filling
- round biscuit cutter or small juice glass
- flat baking tray
- spatula

❶ Roll out the dough so it is 0.5 centimetres thick. Use the biscuit cutter to cut out 5-centimetre circles of dough.

❷ Place the circles of dough on a baking tray.

❸ Prick the dough circles with a fork to stop them puffing while cooking.

❹ Bake at 350 °F (180 °C, gas mark 4) until the moon cakes are slightly puffed, a light golden brown colour, and cooked through.

❺ Remove the baking tray from the oven and leave to cool.

❻ Use a spatula to move the moon cakes to a plate.

❼ Spread jam or other filling on one moon cake and top it with another moon cake.

Moon cakes

Moon cakes can be eaten as part of a celebration.

Activity: Make an abacus

It is hard to imagine counting without numbers, but there was a time when written numbers did not exist. An abacus helped shopkeepers and other people keep track of large numbers. Many cultures used abacuses, but the abacus we are most familiar with today was invented by the Chinese.

Warning!

Make sure you read all the directions before beginning the project.

Supplies

- 6 ice-lolly sticks
- 3 additional lolly sticks (optional)
- 56 plastic beads, large enough for the the dowel rods to pass through
- 3 0.25 cm-diameter dowel rods (available at DIY stores) each approximately 30 cm long
- pencil
- glue

The ancient Chinese used an abacus to do sums.

1 Ask an adult to help you break your dowel rods into thirds. It is possible to cut the dowel rods with strong classroom scissors. Or, you could ask an adult to score them with a knife where you want the cuts to be, and carefully break each dowel rod where it is scored.

2 Place a lolly stick on your work surface. Place the ends of eight dowel rods along the lolly stick, equally spaced. Mark their places with a pencil, and remove the dowel rods. (See Picture A)

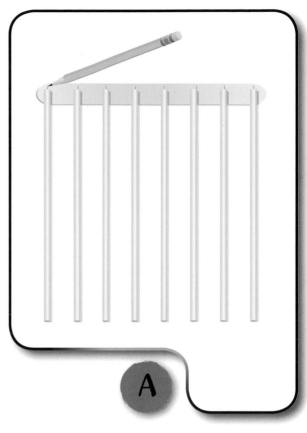

A

3 Carefully squeeze glue onto your pencil lines. Put the dowel rod ends back into position in the glue. Let the glue dry.

4 After the glue dries, thread two beads on to each dowel rod. These are the "heaven beads". Each "heaven bead" represents a unit of five.

5 Place a second lolly stick underneath the dowel rods. Leave some room between this stick and the beads so that you have room to move the beads back and forth between the lolly sticks. This new stick will separate the "heaven beads" from the "earth beads" in step 7. (See Picture B)

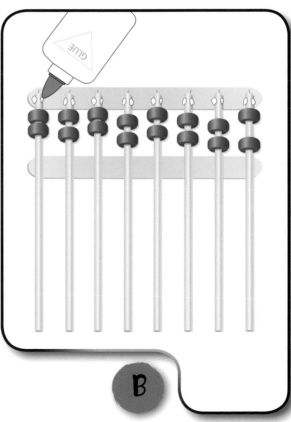

B

6 Mark the positions of the dowel rods on the second lolly stick with a pencil. Once again, glue the dowel rods to the lolly stick where you made these marks. Don't accidentally glue the beads so that they can't move!

7 After the glue has dried, thread five beads on to each dowel rod. These are the "earth beads". Each "earth bead" represents a unit of one. (See Picture C)

8 Place a third lolly stick under the tips of the dowel rods. Again, mark their positions with a pencil, and glue the dowel rods in place.

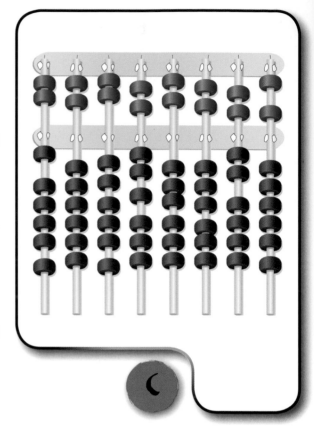

C

9 While the glue is drying, place another lolly stick over the dowel rods at the other end, covering your first stick, and sandwiching the dowel rods in between. Make sure the two lolly sticks are lined up, then carefully glue the new stick down on to the dowel rods. (See Picture D)

10 Repeat this process on the second and third lolly sticks, gluing new sticks to the dowel rods so that they are sandwiched between the lolly sticks.

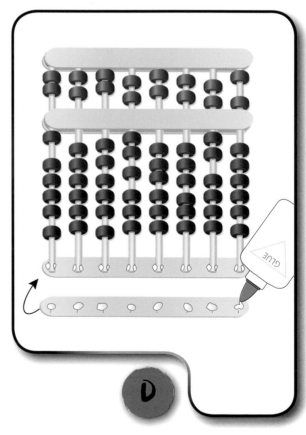

D

11 If you want to be able to move the beads more easily, glue additional lolly sticks to the bottom side of your abacus so that the beads are suspended above the work surface.

⬆ Abacus

You can use your finished abacus to help solve maths problems.

How do you think you use an abacus to do sums? After coming up with your own theory, you could look online, or in a reference book for the answer.

Activity: Make paper

The ancient Chinese invented paper and made it by pressing tree bark and cloth rags together. You can make your own paper out of old newspapers.

Warning!

This is a messy project; protect your clothes and work surfaces.

Ask an adult to use the blender. Read all the directions before beginning the project.

In ancient China, paper was made from tree bark and cloth rags.

Supplies
- papermaking screen
- assorted recyclable paper
- electric blender
- deep plastic tray or dish, or a washing-up bowl large enough to hold the papermaking screen
- folded kitchen towels, recyclable newspapers, or paper towels
- spatula
- rolling pin
- baking tray
- 2 tsp starch (optional)
- glitter, confetti, or dried flowers (optional)
- hairdryer (optional)

A note on supplies:
This project requires a papermaking screen. There are several ways to make screen. Fine nylon net or mesh (or even old, clean tights) can be placed over the inside part of an embroidery hoop. Then attach the outer hoop, with the "screen" side up. You can also staple your chosen screening to an old picture frame to make a more permanent papermaking screen.

This project is a great opportunity to use leftover scraps of paper from other projects. Or use paper towels, tissue paper, or newspaper — but not the shiny paper used in advertising leaflets, etc.

1 Tear the scraps of paper into pieces about the size of postage stamps. Keep in mind that mixing colours of paper is like mixing colours of paint, so choose which colours you mix carefully.

2 Pour 250 millilitres of warm water into the blender. Place scraps of paper into the blender loosely until they are almost to the top of the blender. Do not pack down the paper.

3 With the lid on, ask an adult to turn the blender on at its lowest setting. If there appears to be too much paper, turn the blender off, and add a little more water, and try again. If you still need more water, ask the adult to continue to add water until the blender turns. The mixture should be the consistency of porridge or apple sauce. This process separates the wood fibres. Papermakers call this mixture pulp. If you are going to write on this paper, ask an adult to mix two teaspoons of starch into this mixture.

4 Fold the kitchen towels, paper towels, or newspapers into a pad about 2.5 centimetres thick and about the same size as your screen. This pad is called a couching mound. Put it on your work surface. Place a baking tray under it if you need to keep the work surface dry.

5 Place the screen flat on the bottom of the plastic bowl or deep tray. Make sure the screen side of the frame is facing up. (See picture A)

A

6 Carefully pour the pulp from the blender on to the screen. Try to cover the screen evenly. If you see a lot of holes in your paper, pour the pulp back into the blender, and add more paper. Keep mixing in enough paper so that the pulp is thick enough to stick to the surface of the screen.

7 When the pulp has had a minute or two to drain on the screen, carefully move the screen to the couching mound.

8 In one quick motion, turn the screen over onto the couching mound. Slowly and carefully rock the screen from one edge to the other to loosen the paper on to the couching mound. You can also use a spatula to separate the paper from the screen. (See Picture B)

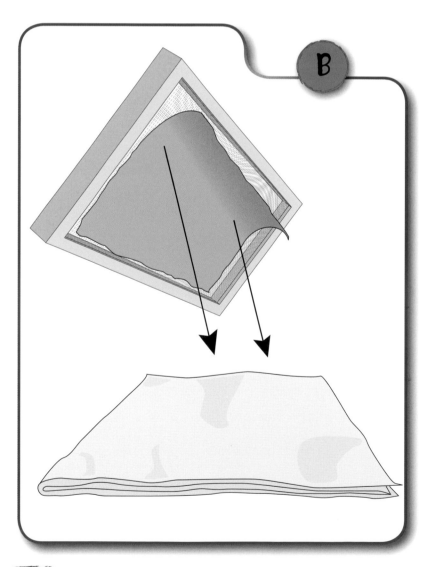

B

9 Place a towel or layer of paper towels over your paper sheet. Use a rolling pin to carefully press out more water. Gently remove the top towel, and move your new paper to where it can dry. If it looks as if it will tear, leave it on the top towel of your couching mound. Then move the towel and paper together to a sunny place, or use a hairdryer to dry it more quickly.

10 Finished sheets can be hung on a clothesline to finish drying.

⑪ Once you have learned the process, try adding different materials to your pulp.

Home-made paper

Your finished project can now be used to make a card for a parent or friend.

Cotton fibres, cardboard egg carton pieces, shredded comic pages, confetti, dried flowers, or glitter could be added to the pulp or to the surface of the damp sheet before it dries. What will adding these materials do to your paper?

Activity: Do the tiger walk

Many Chinese exercises imitate the movements of animals. The ancient Chinese respected the tiger. According to the Chinese calendar, those born in the year of the tiger are sensitive and short-tempered.

The purpose of the tiger walk exercise is to improve movement in your spine and hips.

The tiger was a respected animal in ancient China.

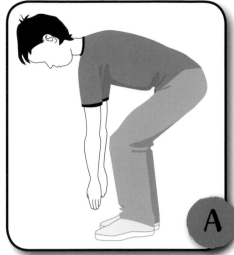

1. Stand with your feet shoulder-width apart.

2. Bend your body forward, and bend your knees so that your back is almost parallel with the floor. (See Picture A)

3. Grab your left ankle with your left hand, and your right ankle with your right hand. (See Picture B)

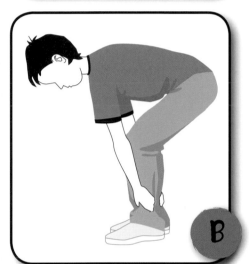

4. Take a step forward with the right foot, while turning your head to the right. (See Picture C)

5. Take a step forward with your left foot, while turning your head to the left.

6. Walk eight steps in this position.

7. Release your ankles and return to standing position.

8. Repeat exercise two to four times.

As you were doing the tiger walk, you were low to the ground like a tiger. Did you see the room as a tiger might see it?

Glossary

archaeologist person who studies the remains of past cultures

civilization literature, traditions, customs, religious, and physical structures of a particular people at a particular time

dynasty families who rule an area for more than one generation

nomad person who moves around from place to place following a food supply

philosophy way of thinking about the world

taxes fee paid to a ruler or government

More books to read

Ancient China, Philip Steele (Anness Publishing, 2002)

Arts and Crafts of the Ancient World: Ancient China, Ting Morris (Watts Publishing, 2006)

Exploring Continents: Asia, Bob Kettle (Heinemann Library, 2006)

World of Recipes: China, Julie McCulloch (Heinemann Library, 2001)

World Tour: China, Noelle Morris (Raintree, 2004)

The instructions for the crafts and activities are designed to allow pupils to work as independently as possible. However, it is always a good idea to make a prototype before assigning any project so that pupils can see how their own work will look when completed. Prior to introducing these activities, teachers should collect and prepare the materials and be ready for any modifications that may be necessary. Participating in the project-making process will help teachers understand the directions and be ready to assist pupils with difficult steps. Teachers might also choose to adapt or modify the projects to better suit the needs of an individual child or class. No one knows the levels of achievement pupils will reach better than their teacher.

While it is preferable for pupils to work as independently as possible, there is some flexibility in regards to project materials and tools. They can vary according to what is available. For instance, while standard white glue may be most familiar, there might be times when a teacher will choose to speed up a project by using a hot glue gun to join materials. Where plaster gauze is not availabe, papier mâché can often be used. Likewise, while a project may call for leather cord, in most instances it is possible to substitute plastic rope or even wool or string. Acrylic paint may be recommended because it adheres better to a material like felt or plastic, but other types of paint would be suitable as well. Circles can be drawn with a compass, or simply by tracing a cup, roll of tape, or other circular object. Allowing pupils a broad spectrum of creativity and opportunities to problem-solve within the parameters of a given project will encourage their critical thinking skills most fully.

Each project contains a question within the directions. These questions are meant to be thought-provoking and promote discussion while pupils work on the project.

Index